My Religion and Me
We are
HINDUS

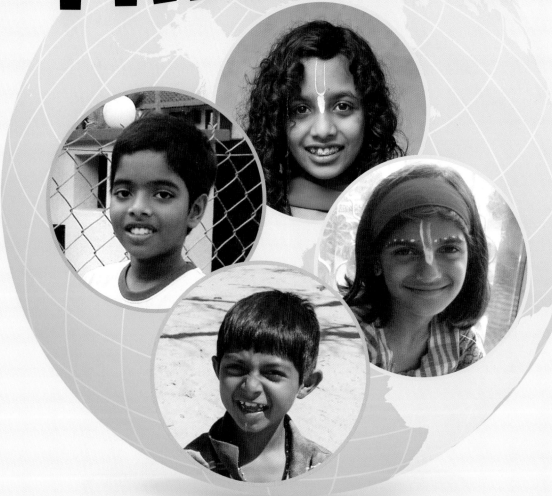

Philip Blake

W
FRANKLIN WATTS
LONDON • SYDNEY

Franklin Watts
338 Euston Road
London, NW1 3BH

Franklin Watts Australia
Level 17/207 Kent Street
Sydney, NSW 2000

Series designed and created for Franklin Watts by Storeybooks.

Acknowledgements
The Publisher would like to thank Jasmine, Nimai, Abishek and Shivanjali as well
as Bhaktivedanta Manor Hare Krishna Temple, Watford for their help in
producing this book.

Faith advisor: Rasamandala Das

Photo credits: Alamy p27; I-stock p4 (top), 9 (top), 11 (top),17, 19 (top and
middle) and 21; Tudor Photography p3 (bottom right), 4 (bottom) 5, 6 (bottom)
8, 9 (bottom), 12, 13, 14 and 15.
Additional photographs were supplied by the children featured in the book which,
despite their best efforts, may not always be of the highest quality.
Every attempt has been made to clear copyright. Should there be any inadvertent
omission please apply to the publisher for rectification.

Dewey number: 294.5

ISBN: 978 1 4451 3889 3

Printed in Malaysia

Franklin Watts is a division of Hachette Children's Books,
an Hachette UK company. www.hachette.co.uk

Note:
The opinions expressed in this book are personal to the children
we talked to and all opinions are subjective and can vary.

Contents

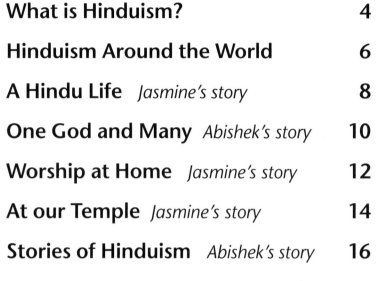

Words in **bold** can be found in the glossary.

What is Hinduism?

Hinduism is a religion that began in India about 5,000 years ago. It has no single founder or prophet and draws on many different sacred texts. It is more about how people live their lives than about their beliefs.

A faith of many gods

The Hindu faith is unusual among religions because it has no standard set of beliefs, so it is followed in different ways by different believers. For example, in Hinduism there are many gods. Some Hindus are devoted to one particular god or goddess, others to several, but most believe that all these **deities** are aspects of one Supreme Being.

▲ The elephant-headed Ganesh, "remover of all obstacles", is one of the most popular of all Hindu gods.

Hindu temples vary in appearance according to where they are located. This is Jasmine's temple in Oxfordshire, England. ▶

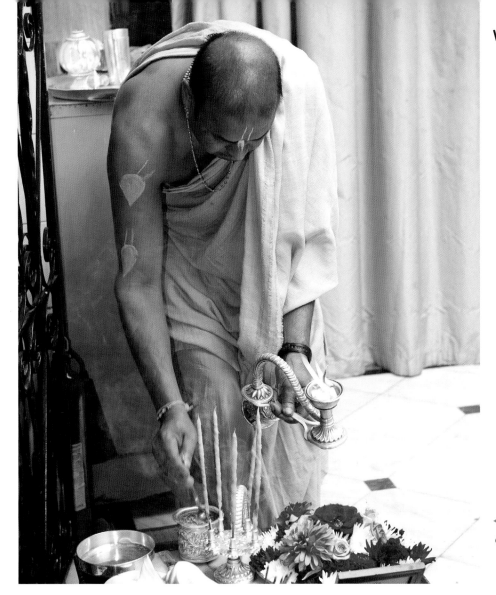

◀ *A priest makes an offering at an altar.*

Karma

One thing that all Hindus have in common is a belief that they are all part of a continuous process of life, death and rebirth. A moral law called the law of **karma** determines how people will be reborn. So living and behaving well creates good karma and favourable rebirth but actions that harm others lead to bad karma.

Shared values

Hindus also share many values. They honour the importance of the family, paying special respect to their elders. They try to be kind to other living things and avoid violence. Many Hindus are vegetarians.

Hinduism Around the World

Having begun in India long ago, Hinduism has flourished and developed there ever since. The religion has also spread around the world as Indian people have travelled and taken their beliefs with them.

India and beyond

Today there are at least 900 million Hindus living on the **Indian subcontinent**. There is probably a similar number spread around the rest of the world. These Hindus are mostly in places where there are large Indian populations, including Britain. In addition, a number of more recent groups, such as the International Society for **Krishna** Consciousness (**ISKCON**) founded in the 20th century, have carried Hindu ideas far and wide and converted many people to the faith.

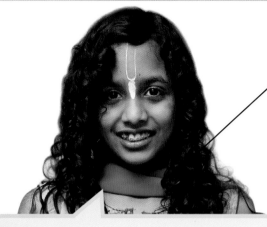

I am Nimai. I live in Germantown, Maryland, USA and I am nine years old. I live with my father, a software engineer, and my mother, a homemaker. My grandparents live in Assam, India, and I visit them every year. I am educated at home and I enjoy art and music. I am learning the flute, harmonium, sarod (an Indian stringed instrument) and mrdanga (an Indian clay drum). I also love reading stories such as the **Mahabharata**, the **Ramayana** and *Harry Potter*.

My name is Jasmine and I live in Wheatley, near Oxford in England. I live with my parents and my sister, Janaki, who is 14 years old, and my brother, Nikhil, who is eight years old. I go to the local secondary school. I enjoy sports such as running and tennis and I really like trampolining. I also enjoy going to Krishna Club.

My name is Abishek. I am 11 years old and live in Bangsar, a suburb of Kuala Lumpur, the capital of Malaysia. I live with my parents and my sister, Aishwarya, who is a year younger than me. I play plenty of football and **futsal** and I am a keen reader. At school, I am a prefect, head of the cadet corps and I play chess and enter science competitions for my school. I also enjoy playing the piano, learning Indian classical music, surfing the Internet and playing games on my computer.

I am Shivanjali and I live in the city of Pune, in India's Maharashtra State. I am ten years old and I go to the St Felix High School in Pune. I live with my parents and my four-year-old brother, Vishwambhar. The hobbies I enjoy most are reading, singing and dancing. I also like acting in plays.

In this book, four children share their experiences of life in Hindu families in different parts of the world. It is important to remember that other Hindus will have different opinions and experiences of their own faith.

7

A Hindu Life
Jasmine's story

▲ *Me and my family at home in England.*

As Hindus, we try to live as good a life as we can. Our religion shapes every part of our lives, especially the way we treat others and everyday matters, such as the kind of food we eat.

Respect for elders

I am always expected to respect my elders – my parents, grandparents, teachers and older people generally. If I was sitting on a bench and an elderly person was standing because there was no room to sit down, I would give up my seat for them.

Foods

I am not allowed to eat some foods, such as meat, fish or eggs, because Hinduism teaches us to be kind to animals. But foods such as milk, butter and **ghee** are good from a religious viewpoint, because they come from cows, which we believe to be holy.

Cleanliness

In our family, my mum prepares the food. Before she does any cooking she has a bath and puts on clean clothes and she washes her hands regularly while working in the kitchen. When preparing meals for the murtis (holy images) she uses different utensils and cleaning equipment from those used for our own food.

The sacred cow

In Hindu culture, the cow is sacred because it is believed to be one of the **seven mothers** as it produces milk with which people make butter and ghee. Hindus believe that the bull represents the father as it ploughs the fields that produce grains for us to eat.

▲ *A cow rests by the side of the road in India, where cows are allowed to wander freely.*

▼ *I help my mum prepare our food in the kitchen.*

One God and Many
Abishek's story

T he Hindu religion is known for having many gods and goddesses. We see all these deities as parts or aspects of one larger reality, which we call Brahman. Most Hindus have several deities in their shrine, but they often have one favourite god to whom they are especially devoted.

A favourite god

My favourite god is Lord Ganesh, who is one of the sons of Lord Shiva and goddess Parvati. He has the head of an elephant and a huge stomach. He is known as the remover of all obstacles, so many people pray to him when they are starting a new project or facing a new challenge.

Major gods

Three of our most important gods are Lord Brahma, Lord Vishnu and

▲ I sit and pray in front of our shrine at home.

This is a statue ▶ of Lord Ganesh.

Lord Shiva. Lord Brahma is the creator of living beings. He has four heads and sits on a water lily. Lord Vishnu is the protector of living beings. He lies on a serpent and has a chakra (disc) around his finger. Lord Shiva is the destroyer of living beings. He is dark-skinned, has three eyes, holds a trident and has a tiger skin around his neck.

Shiva or Vishnu?

Most Hindus are either Shaivites, who worship Lord Shiva, or Vaishnavites, who see Lord Vishnu as the Supreme One. However, I have images of both Lord Shiva and Lord Vishnu in my shrine.

Some Hindu deities
Brahma, the Creator
Shiva, the Destroyer
Vishnu, the Preserver or Protector
Krishna, the Supreme Lord, **avatar** of
   Vishnu
Ganesh, the Remover of Obstacles
Hanuman, the Monkey-God
Lakshmi, the goddess of wealth and
   good fortune.

Jasmine says:
There are pictures of gods and goddesses everywhere in my house, including my bedroom. We have a big picture of the deities in our hallway.

▼ *My sister and I are standing in front of a shrine with a statue of Lord Shiva at our temple.*

Worship at Home
Jasmine's story

▲ *In front of our home shrine are flowers that we have offered to the deities.*

At home I have a shrine that has lots of pictures and statues of deities – Radha, Krishna, Sita, Laxman, Hanuman, Gaua-Nitai and Ganesh. There are also pictures of members of our family who have passed away and a picture of Prabhuppada, the founder of ISKCON. There is space in front of the shrine where we can sit on a cushion to **pray or** meditate.

Morning offerings

Every morning my mother blows the **conch** to signal that **arti** – the ceremony at which we make offerings to the deities – is about to begin and we should all come down to the shrine. She offers fruit and water, incense, and then the arti itself. Then she takes a conch shell filled with water and offers this to the deities to wash their feet, followed by a cloth to dry them. At the end of the ceremony she offers flowers to the deities.

The evening ceremony

In the evening we hold another arti ceremony. This time my mum wraps the deities in their blankets and closes the blinds of the shrine. Then we sing songs and meditate for a while.

Caring for the deities

We care for the deities by dusting and bathing them regularly. We also change the deities' clothes and replace anything on the shrine that is damaged so that the shrine is pure and clean.

▲ *My mother blows the conch shell. Its sound is a signal that the arti ceremony is about to start.*

▼ *My mother makes an offering of light.*

13

At our Temple
Jasmine's story

▲ *Many offerings of food are made at our temple.*

Before going to worship at our temple, we all prepare by having a shower. This is to ensure that we are clean and pure. When we arrive at the temple we show our devotion to the deities by bowing down low on the floor.

The temple deities

The deities at the temple are cared for carefully and bathed regularly, just like the deities in our shrine at home. The deities are dressed in colourful Indian clothing with pretty patterns. They wear flower garlands, earrings, bracelets, necklaces and crowns. Krishna also has a flute.

Making offerings

At the temple, offerings are made to the deities. Many different things are offered, including perfumes, oils, flowers, fruit, food and Tulsi, the basil plant that is sacred because it is associated with the goddess Lakshmi. We also offer food to the deities to be blessed. We eat this food, which we call **Prasad**, afterwards.

Religious music

Singing and music are an important part of the temple ritual. We sing religious songs, hymns and the Hare Krishna **mantra**. The singing is called **kirtan** and is accompanied by music on instruments such as the mrdanga (drums) and a harmonica and flute, while the main singer sings. We clap the rhythm and follow the song that is being sung.

▲ *We take blessings after the priest has offered arti to the deities.*

◀ *A musician at the temple plays the mrdanga.*

The Hare Krishna mantra

Made up of the names Hare, Krishna and Rama, the Hare Krishna mantra is a sixteen-word sacred text repeated by devotees to Lord Krishna. It was made popular outside India by ISKCON, the religious organization that is widely known as the "Hare Krishna Movement".

Stories of Hinduism
Abishek's story

▲ *I am reading the* Ramayana, *the story of Lord Rama and Sita.*

There are many stories about the thousands of Hindu gods. A favourite story is called the *Ramayana.* This is the story of Lord Rama, an Indian prince, who is also one of the ten incarnations or avatars of Vishnu, and his devoted wife, Sita. The *Ramayana* is a long poem, but its story has been retold in many books, plays and films.

In the forest

Rama was the son of King Dasaratha and the rightful heir to the throne. But Rama was banished to the forest for 14 years because the king decided that, as a favour to his youngest wife, her son

> *Nimai says:*
> I've read the *Ramayana* a few times. I like the part where Hanuman jumps over the ocean to find Sita.

> *Jasmine says:*
> In our shrine at home Rama, Sita and Hanuman sit together.

Shatrughna would become king instead of Rama. When Rama went into exile, his wife Sita and brother Lakshmana followed him. One day, when the brothers were hunting a deer, Sita was kidnapped by Ravana, the evil king of Lanka.

Helpers of Rama

It was difficult to rescue Sita, as Ravana kept her prisoner in Lanka. But Rama was helped by the Monkey-King Sugriva, who offered his army to attack Lanka and save Sita. They were also helped by Hanuman, the monkey-god, who stands for devotion, selflessness, loyalty, strength and valour.

The rescue of Sita

Hanuman used his powers and quick wits to help Rama attack Lanka and rescue Sita. When the monkey army was unable to get across the sea to Lanka, Hanuman made himself really big and flew across the sea. When Ravana set Hanuman's dangling tail on fire with a burning cloth, Hanuman made his tail longer and spread the blaze. Later, Ravana was defeated and Rama could rescue Sita.

► This is a statue of the monkey-god, Hanuman.

Divali

Nimai's story

▲ I remember celebrating Divali at my grandparents' home in India. I especially enjoyed the firecrackers.

In the Hindu month of Ashwin, which falls in September or October, we celebrate Divali. Divali is one of the most popular Hindu festivals. It is a fun time when there are special decorations and parties but it is also a time for worship and thinking about our beliefs.

Lord Rama's festival

Divali is associated with Lord Rama, because this is the time when he returned to his kingdom of Ayodhya in northeastern India. To celebrate, the people who lived there decorated their houses with lamps and today Divali is the festival of light.

> ### *Abishek says:*
> Rama is one of the avatars or incarnations of Lord Vishnu. He shows Hindus how to distinguish right and wrong and also teaches us about the equality between man and woman.

▲ *A statue of the goddess Lakshmi.*

Decorations and celebrations

We prepare for Divali by cleaning our house thoroughly. Then we put up decorations, especially lots of lights. Some people make special clay lamps, but my parents and I buy candles from the store. In our family we celebrate Divali by holding a party. My mom makes delicious food and we invite people and have a nice gathering. We also worship and talk about Lord Rama.

Lakshmi and Divali

The goddess Lakshmi is the deity who is especially linked with Divali. The **consort** of Vishnu and goddess of fortune and wealth, she brings wealth to people's houses and showers good fortune on people who live a holy life and who serve God.

▼ *On Divali night, the front door of our home was decorated with banana tree trunks, lamps (inset) and colourful markings on the ground.*

Holi

Shivanjali's story

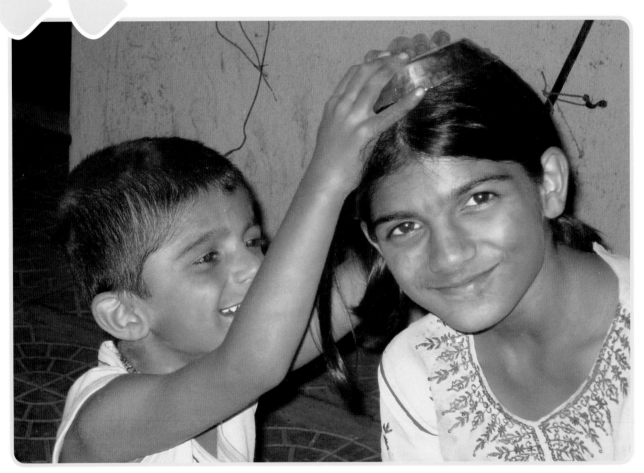

▲ *At Holi we all get covered in coloured dye.*

We celebrate the festival of Holi during the Hindu month of Phalgun, which usually falls in March. Holi is linked to the new year, harvest time and events in the life of Lord Krishna.

Festive foods

At Holi, people celebrate by eating a variety of festive foods such as sweets, savouries and all kinds of things that are good to eat. Even vegetarians, who keep to the restrictions of their diet, like to enjoy themselves by eating more than usual.

20

A colourful time

At Holi, people throw or spray coloured dyes at each other. This is a way of marking the victory over evil and the coloured dyes stand for love and friendship. This custom began after Krishna defeated a demon called Shankchuda. He celebrated with his brother Balaram, his sister Subhadra and all the boys and girls who worked as cowherds by spraying gulal or red dye over each other.

Spring and harvest

In India, the time of Holi is the beginning of spring, the season when it is neither too hot nor too cold. Farmers are especially thankful because this is the time when they harvest their crops, so Holi is a time when they celebrate a good harvest.

Lord Krishna

The Lord Krishna is an avatar of the god Vishnu, in other words he is one of the forms in which Vishnu came to earth in order to defeat evil. He is seen as a source of wisdom, as a gentle husband to his consort, Radha, and, by many, as the Supreme Being.

Nimai says:
I've spent Holi in India a couple of times. I enjoyed throwing coloured powder on my parents.

▲ Powder is made in all kinds of bright colours.

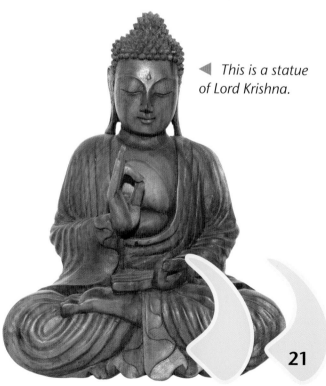

◄ *This is a statue of Lord Krishna.*

21

Special Journeys
Nimai's story

▲ *I enjoyed my bath in a holy pond in Vrindavan.*

Many Hindus go on special journeys called pilgrimages, to visit places in India that are closely linked to our religion and deities. My parents and I went on a pilgrimage to Vrindavan, the place in India where the Supreme Lord Krishna appeared.

Pilgrimage to Vrindavan

To go to Vrindavan, we travelled by aeroplane from Washington to Delhi and then took a taxi to Vrindavan. There were thousands of other pilgrims in Vrindavan – the place is always packed with visitors, whether or not it is festival time. In Vrindavan we especially enjoyed visiting the beautiful ancient temples in which Krishna, the Supreme Personality of the Godhead, and his consort Radha are worshipped.

◄ *We visited this beautiful gate in Ekachakra, West Bengal, which is a site many Hindus go to on pilgrimage.*

During my travels, I received a book on Ramanujacharya, a famous teacher from the 10th century, from his Holiness Chandramanli Swami of ISKCON. ▶

Festivals and pilgrimages

There are many other places of pilgrimage in India and there are special festivals, such as Janmashtami (celebrating the birth of Lord Krishna) and Govardhan Puja (worship of the sacred mountain Govardhan, near Mathura in Uttar Pradesh in India), when many people make a special journey to one of the holy places.

The Ganges

Many people make a pilgrimage to the River Ganges. The Ganges is the most sacred river in Hinduism and is said to flow from the feet of Vishnu himself. When you bathe in the River Ganges, all your sins are washed away. Coming into contact with the waters is a way of receiving the river's devotion to the Supreme Lord.

Jasmine says:
Karma means the result of your actions, good or bad. For example it is said you get good karma from going on a pilgrimage, bad karma from eating the meat of a cow.

Naming a Baby
Shivanjali's story

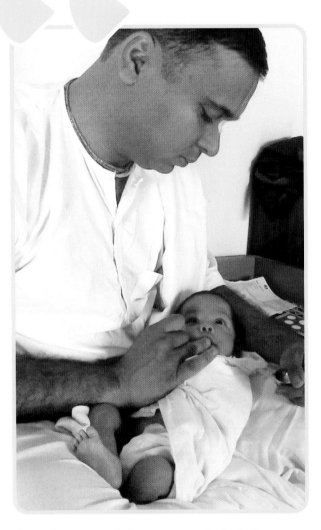

▲ *Father puts a little honey on the baby's tongue.*

▲ *He recites the Maha mantra in the baby's ear.*

When my brother was born, my father put a mixture of ghee and honey on his tongue, to protect him and to give him intelligence. Our father then whispered a sacred mantra into my brother's ears.

24

The naming ceremony

A few days after my brother was born, there was a naming ceremony, led by our family **guru**, at our home. On this day, lots of our relatives came to give their blessings and to bring gifts for my brother. They rocked the baby and sang many hymns including songs about the birds, the moon and a lullaby to send him to sleep. After he had been given his name, we all enjoyed the delicious food that my mother prepared for the occasion.

Looking to the future

Hindu parents usually ask their guru to draw up their child's **horoscope**. This is important as a guide to the child's future. Some families use the guidance of **astrology** to choose the child's name, but in others, the wishes of the parents are followed.

Early days

At the time of the naming ceremony, my brother still had not been out of doors. Babies are usually kept indoors for at least 30 to 40 days, as they are not ready to be exposed to the outside environment. After that time, my parents took him to the temple to have the **darshan** of the Lord.

Darshan

The name darshan ("seeing") is used for an important part of Hindu worship in which the worshipper comes before the temple deity to offer prayers and be seen. People also speak of "having darshan" with a guru or religious teacher.

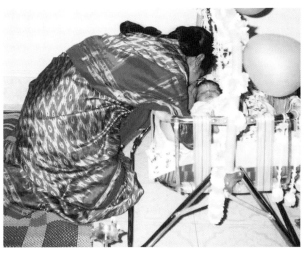

▲ *At a special ceremony the women of the family recite the Maha mantra in the boy's ears ...*
▼ *and give **adornments** to the child.*

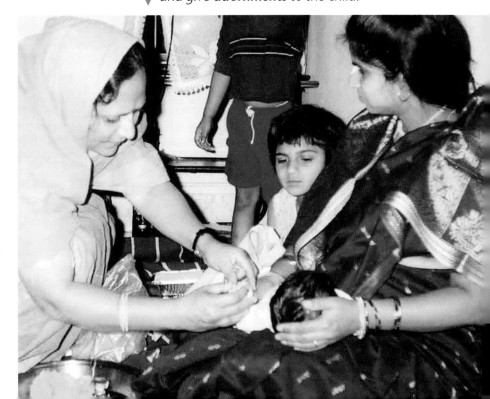

The Sacred Thread Ceremony
Shivanjali's story

◀ *This picture was taken at the Sacred Thread Ceremony of a friend of ours. There was a special meal to celebrate the occasion.*

The Sacred Thread Ceremony marks the point when a boy begins his formal religious education under a spiritual master or guru. I went to the ceremony when the son of one of my father's friends was given his sacred thread.

The thread

The sacred thread is made of strands of cotton. A thread usually contains three, five or seven strands. Being given the sacred thread shows people that the wearer is ready to begin formal education, so the ceremony usually takes place when the child is about eight years old.

Giving the thread

A brahmana (priest) led the ceremony. At the beginning, he performed chants and mantras. Then the boy was given the sacred thread, which his spiritual master placed on his left side. He will wear this thread until he formally accepts a vow of initiation from his spiritual master.

A lasting sign

The thread ceremony is a sign that the person is committed to accept the teachings of a guru. The person will wear a sacred thread for the rest of his life.

Abishek says:
The three strands of a sacred thread represent Gayatri (goddess of mind), Saraswati (goddess of word) and Savitri (goddess of deed). They also remind the person of his debt to his guru, his parents and to society.

▼ *The boy is ready to receive his sacred thread.*

Glossary

adornment A decoration worn on the body such as a piece of jewellery.

arti A form of worship involving devotion to a deity that is expressed with offerings and, especially, the use of a ghee lamp.

astrology The study of how the stars and planets are said to influence our lives.

avatar One of the forms that a deity, especially Vishnu, may take when visiting Earth.

Brahman The supreme reality, of which everything, including all the gods and goddesses, forms a part.

conch A kind of tropical shell that makes a musical sound when blown.

consort A husband or wife of a deity.

darshan Part of worship in which a person is seen by a deity and receives their blessing.

deity A god or goddess.

futsal Indoor football.

ghee Specially prepared, or clarified, butter used in religious rituals as well as in Indian medicine and cooking.

guru A religious teacher or leader.

horoscope A chart showing the positions of the planets and stars when a person is born; used to predict their future or make suggestions about how they should live their lives.

Indian subcontinent The geographical area including India, Nepal, Pakistan, and nearby islands, such as Sri Lanka.

ISKCON The International Society for Krishna Consciousness, a religious organisation that teaches awareness of Krishna; widely known as the Hare Krishna movement.

karma The idea that all actions have good or bad effects or consequences, and that the consequences of people's actions affect the way they are reborn into their next life after they die.

kirtan Chanting of hymns or mantras to the accompaniment of musical instruments, used in temple devotion.

Krishna The eighth avatar of the god Vishnu, worshipped as a god in his own right.

lunar calendar A calendar based on the 28-day phases of the Moon.

Mahabharata A long poem, describing the epic battle between two rival families, along with many other stories.

mantra A sacred syllable, phrase or poem, used in religious ceremonies or during meditation.

meditate A way of concentrating or focusing the mind by emptying it of distracting thoughts and feelings.

Prasad Food offered to a deity and then eaten by the worshippers.

Rama The seventh avatar of the god Vishnu and hero of the Ramayana, worshipped as a god in his own right.

Ramayana A long poem telling the story of Rama, the kidnapping of his wife Sita, and her rescue by Rama with the help of Hanuman.

seven mothers Seven mother-goddesses, traditionally worshipped by women, especially pregnant women or those will small children.

shrine A place, often in someone's house, where images of one or more gods are kept, acting as a focus for worship and devotion.

Further Information

Websites

BBC Religion and Ethics:
www.bbc.co.uk/religion/religions/ hinduism

Religion Facts:
www.religionfacts.com/hinduism/ index.htm

The Heart of Hinduism (ISKCON):
http://hinduism.iskcon.com

The Hindu Year

The Hindu religion follows a lunar calendar and has many festivals celebrating both the changing seasons and events connected with the various deities. Many of these are celebrated by Hindus all over the world, but some are local, celebrating notable regional deities or people. Typical festival days feature extended worship and visits to the temple. Most festivals involve feasting, but some include fasting.

Here a selection of festivals is shown with the Hindu month in which it occurs, together with the equivalent western months.

Holi (Phalgun: February/March)
A time of great merriment and celebration, Holi originated as a harvest festival. Around the world, people celebrate by throwing coloured dyes at each other.

Ram Navami (Chaitra: March/April)
The birthday of Rama is celebrated on

Ram Navami. People eat special foods (although there are also some foods that may not be eaten on this day). The *Ramayana*, containing the story of Rama, is read on this day.

Krishna Janamastami (Bhadrapad: August/September)
This festival celebrates the birthday of Krishna. The baby Krishna is welcomed and people enjoy eating sweet foods. Stories of Krishna are told.

Navaratri or Durga Puja (Ashwin: September/October)
The festival of nine nights, or Navaratri, is a celebration of the goddess Durga. During the evenings people dance around Durga's shrines. Many people fast, limiting themselves to one meal containing sweet foods made with milk each day.

Dussehra (Ashwin: September/October)
Meaning "the tenth", Dussehra occurs at the end of Navaratri. This day marks the defeat of the demon Ravana in the *Ramayana*. His images are carried through the streets and then burned, to represent the defeat of evil by good.

Divali (Kartika: October/November)
During the five-day festival of lights, people decorate their houses and put up many lights. Houses are cleaned, families get together and people enjoy parties.

Index